When My Soul Started To Fly

60 Inspirational poems by

Stephanie A. Young

Library of Congress Cataloging-in-Publication Data

ISBN: 0971123586

Young, Stephanie A.

When My Soul Started To Fly

Copyright © 2015 by Stephanie A. Young

All rights reserved. Printed in the United States of America. Except as permitted under the United States Copyright Act of 1976, no part of this book may be reproduced or transmitted in any form or by any means without written permission of the author.

Cover Design: Destiny Publishings
Photography: Destiny Publishings
Editor: Destiny Publishings
Transcription: Johnathan Young

Dedication

Dedicated to my family and friends who instilled in me the love of God words and adventure of life thank you for being a wonderful part of my world.

Table of Contents

Day 1 - Truly Wonderful 1

Day 2 - Cause Mama Said So, Tina 2

Day 3 - Baby Dreams 4

Day 4 - Mama's Black Baby 5

Day 5 - Diva's House 6

Day 6 - One Funky Note 8

Day 7 - Rhythm and Blues 10

Day 8 - Blues In My Head 12

Day 9 - The Land of the Funk 13

Day 10 - A Tour with Too Many Stars 14

Day 11- I have Won This Race 16

Day 12 - Do You Know What You Just Said? ..17

Day 13 - What Spirit Was That? 18

Day 14 - In God's Name 19

Day 15 - Play Me 20

Day 16 - Silent Kisses 21

Day 17 - Steps to Love 22

Day 18 - Eternal 23

Day 19 - A Fine Man 24

Day 20 - A Fool's Love 25

Day 21 - Gift 26

Day 22 - Happy As I Am 27

Day 23 - The Lust of a Woman 28

Day 24 - Tell Me the Truth 29

Day 25 - Living Arrangements 30

Day 26 - Just a Thought 31

Day 27 - My Private Vampire 32

Day 28 - Time to Finish the Beginning 34

Day 29 - Night Wish 35

Day 30 - Us 36

Day 31 - Endless Ribbons of Life 37

Day 32 – Dark Side 38

Day 33 - Just Business 39

Day 34 - Word Journey 40

Day 35 - A Ten Dollar Visit 42

Day 36 - Ageless Veil 43

Day 37 - Old Girl 44

Day 38 - Old News..45

Day 39 - Pain in My House 46

Day 40 - Tell Me Who Owns You 47

Day 41 - Unrest...48

Day 42 - Mary, Do You See What You Got? 49

Day 43 - Pathfinders 50

Day 44 - My Name Is Color................................51

Day 45 - Mother of Words 52

Day 46 - Mama's Cooking 53

Day 47 - I know Who I Was................................54

Day 48 - So What If I Got Bills? 55

Day 49 - Just Another Joker 56

Day 50 – Hey! …How Are You?.......................58

Day 51 - My Sister, My Brother.........................60

***Day** 52- World* 61

***Day** 53 - Me and the Gang* 62

***Day** 54 - A Good Day* 63

***Day** 55 - The Ghetto That Won't Rub Off* 64

***Day** 56 - Winters Visit* 66

***Day** 57 - A Voice That Carried* 68

***Day** 58 - Now I Know Better* 69

***Day** 59 - Gathering Of Our Hearts* 70

***Day** 60 - Blessed* 71

Day 1 - Truly Wonderful

"From Minds of a Child"

Why is it so simple for
a small child to see the
beauty in every raindrop
that falls,
every heart that beats,
soul that weeps,
love the searches,
child that believes,
every mouth that prays,
last dance that never ends,
first kiss that was real,
song that moved your heart.
What a gift and a joy it is
to be able to see the beauty
in everything.

Day 2 - Cause Mama Said So, Tina

"Just Because That's What Little Girls Do"

"Why can't I get my own milk?"
"Because you might drop the glass and hurt yourself."
"Okay, Mama."
"Why can't I pick my own dresses for school?'
"Because you only like to wear summer dresses and its winter."
"Okay, Mama."
"Why can't I play with the dog next-door?"
"Because it hasn't had its shots."
"But Mama, I got mine last year."
"No Tina!"
"Okay Mama."
"Why does the mailman stay so long at Mrs. Webster's house?"
"Because he's giving more than mail."
"What, Mama?"
"Never mind, Tina."
"Mama, can I go outside and play in the snow."
"Maybe later, Tina."
"Okay Mama."

"Mama why does the snow leave so soon?"
"Because Tina, seasons change and little girls grow up and mama doesn't have to answer so many questions."
"Yes Mama; let's go outside and play in snow."
"No Tina."
"But, why?"
"Because mama said so, Tina."

Day 3 - Baby Dreams

"Sweet Summer Dreams"

- *Cottontail bunnies*
- *Chocolate showers*
- *Marshmallow clouds*
- *Fudge pillow for my head*
- *Candy drums beat with peppermint sticks*
- *Orange juice pools to splash*
- *Jelly boats to sink*
- *Peanut butter sunglasses to wear*
- *Strawberry rainfalls across the sugar beach*
- *Lemonade ocean breeze*
    …Blows me to sleep

Day 4 - Mama's Black Baby

"My Black Prince"

So what... you don't have hair like silk or nose like an eagle.
But you know why that is?
Because you got your daddy's hair and your mamas nose.
Long, lean and growing every day.
Sometimes I think, why did you do that?
Was it just to see me blow?
Black, young, and an attitude already that I deal with every day.
I should call you black man.
For someday that's what I hope to be around to see.
Proud, strong, loud and drawing a crowd.
Loving, caring, and teaching.
A new world of understanding.
Thank you for schooling me.

Day 5 - Diva's House

"Ladies First Divas for Life"

Lena, you've been in the storm a long time.
Josephine, dance for me.
Marian, this concerts for you.
Bessie, I don't feel blue no more.
Ella, jazz it up for me
Mahalia, the sparrow is still flying.
Leontyne, this is your house.
Sarah, divine one.
Aretha, clean for life.
Dinah, teach me forever.
Tammy, you sang me over the mountain,
through the river, and out valley.
Mary, I think I know your guy.
Pearl, Bill still didn't come home.
Eartha, what's up kitty?
Patty, you are my friend over the rainbow.
Naomi, black like we.
Nat's, little girl still growing every day.
Whitney, get ready girlfriend.
Gladys, schools not out. Teach on.
Nikki, Billie sees you.

When My Soul Started To Fly

Mariah, sing a little higher.
Anita, it gets better and better.

Day 6 - One Funky Note

"Funky Sounds in My Head"

- *Richard, made me shut up.*
- *Miles, did it with horn.*
- *James, did one crazy slide.*
- *Jimmy, is up there somewhere in a haze.*
- *Marvin, made me go crazy then, now, and forever.*
- *Jackie, only came to me in the midnight hour.*
- *Temps, made me weak until the last note.*
- *O'Jays, made me climb every stairway.*
- *Barry, can make you go lower than you ever wanted to.*
- *Earth, Wind, and Fire, is the seed of my heart.*
- *Frankie, lost me in a maze.*
- *Al, I will never leave you alone.*
- *Sly, will always be my family.*

When My Soul Started To Fly

- *Teddy, is still a bear.*
- *Stevie, I see every song.*
- *Ohio Players, don't ever stop the roller coaster.*
- *George, be the dog of your heart.*
- *Cameo, one jewel I will wear until the end.*
- *Michael, can dance all night for me.*
- *Luther, you will always have the power.*
- *Prince, I got the purple room ready.*

Day 7 - Rhythm and Blues

"If I Could See These Notes"

- *James, until you want to shout.*
- *Ella, goes on and on and on and on.*
- *Miles, makes your mind go to peace.*
- *Anita, whispers to you 365 days of the year.*
- *Luther, you're not a fool for love, shaking hips and lips that find the right spot to get you in trouble.*
- *Sammy, with a never ending echo.*
- *Duke, in the wave bigger than his hair.*
- *BB, I love you just as much as Lucille.*
- *Dizzy, we all took a spin with you.*
- *Ruth, you don't need a star because you are a star. Move me, shake me, but old ill wind don't ever lose me Coldhearted but not too lowdown.*
- *Nat, let me see you smile.*
- *Billy, I see your flower in your hair.*
- *BC, what note is that in?*
- *Satchmo, the roses are still red.*
- *Betty, smooth and silky in the dark.*

Cheated, lied to, forgiven her, touched kissed, lay down law.
- *Bessie, nasty as she wanted to be.*
- *Lena, the Nile is yours.*
- *Al, wrap me in your love.*
- *Josephine, the bananas are still ripe.*
- *Charlie, the birds are flying high.*
I got rhythm that keeps the blues away.

Day 8 - Blues In My Head

"Late Night Bar Creeping"

In the back of
the Dew Drop Inn
plays a sax man.
Blues that renews
my heart of
magic nights
and tragic loves,
until I feel concealed,
in a haze of jellyroll
and muddy water.
At the bar sits
the lady in red
waiting for trouble.
In walks trouble,
looking, too fine.
As the night ends
eyes have met,
lips have lied.
Last call for alcohol.

Day 9 - The Land of the Funk

"Music for My Heart and Soul"

To the land I go.
To the land of the funk.
Swing it like an
old Mary Jane in my
left back pocket.
Jazz was the road.
Blues was the path of
the my mind's eye.
I couldn't see the forest
for the trees.
The gospel truth always
sets my heart free.
So I know where
I'm coming from,
and I won't have to go
back to the river again.
Still waters flood of my heart.
But the rain washes
away the pain.
For it is now I go
into the midnight hour.

Day 10 - A Tour with Too Many Stars

"Stars That Shine Forever"

Prince was trippin', sayin', someone had been trying on his outfits.

I said, "You need stop lying, nobody on the bus can wear size (00) but you."

Michael and Stevie we're driving everybody crazy with their water bombs and pies in the face.

James says that he needs two more rollers like 200 wasn't enough for a 10 city tour; not to count the curling irons.

Luther said he was missing a bottle for oil sheen. We all told him to follow his drips backward and leave us alone.

Bobby was hogging the phone and it didn't sound like you know who.

Janet was the only girl on the tour. She told Michael and Stevie they were working on her last nerve.

Elton was the only white boy he told everybody to do their own weave check.
 Little Richard told him, "I bought it with my own money so shut up!"

Eddie and A-man was in everybody's business, but they didn't know we had a tape recorder in the room for the whole tour.

Johnny and Keith close the tour and everybody went home with a few dollars and a few new friends.

Day 11 - I have Won This Race

"A Race We All Have To Run"

An
unseeing mind,
unhearing heart;
I can take the pain
of past
    present
        future.
Daylight comes and
my work is unending.
Nightfall calls and I Pray
I stand in judgment,
not by them and they
but by He.
Just to behold His face,
I'll know, I have won this race.

Day 12 - Do You Know What You Just Said?

"Still Things to Learn"

*The other day a lady told me that
she didn't understand why people
lie to their children about God.
I said, "What do you mean?"
She said, "You know if you do
Everything that God ask of you
no harm will come to you."
I thought, "she really didn't understand."
Did she know that the faith of a child is
a test of love far greater than the world?
Didn't she understand that
God doesn't push you off the cliff?
But you have to jump in his arms
 all on your own.
Do we know so much that we give
so little to others?
Do we travel so far but get nowhere at all?
I have looked for love, but had it all the time.
Now is my time of giving. I shall never stop.*

Day 13 - What Spirit Was That?

"Just Believe"

*The spirit that
no one can stop.
Born to free my soul,
to open our hearts
and minds.
The Spirit that was
used and abused;
never understood
because the dream of
peace was true.
The spirit that
God's child could see.
The future of you and me.
You died for what I now
believe, lives inside of me.*

Day 14 - In God's Name

"He's Alive"

War, that is never ending,
peace, unseen by millions,
prayers, love, and joy,
which no one has time for.

Life, living, and death,
we all must do at least one.
Time winning hearts,
losing loves,
memories of better times
places, and thoughts.

On this summer eve,
peace be still.
For all hearts are listening
in the name of God.

Day 15 - Play Me

"My Heartbeat"

Like an old-school drum
with one drop of rain;

In this beat there is a pulse
that drips and melts away my fear,
shaking, pulling me closer to
where I know I have to be.

The pain is the one thing I can take.

Play me.
   Roll back my lust.
      Grab the last note.
         Now hold it…
            until it will not stop.

Scream for the sound
of my name on your lips.
For the key to it all
is in this everlasting song.

Day 16 - Silent Kisses

"First Love"

From the corner of my eye
to the curve of my shoulder,
fingertip to fingertip, into my
life you creep ever so gently.

You steal my heart until every
drop of blood drips with you.
Strong, but still tender, lasting forever.
Painfully with pleasures to come.

Sweet and tart passion that only
we have learned together.
Whispers on the wind, only my heart
can hear loud and clear.

Even now here in the dark
I can feel your silent kisses
touch me from inside,
as I smile, as I sleep.

Day 17 - Steps to Love

"From 1 to 10 Could All Be Real"

One, the eyes you meet in passing.

*Two, you think all your crazy
dreams are coming true.*

Three, you both make the move of your life.

Four, something always cuts in on you.

Five, the walls are down and off you go.

*Six, reaching for the words. They are just
so mixed they won't come out.*

Seven, one touch and you know it.

Eight, this could be it.

*Nine, no one is in the room
except the two of you.*

*Ten, the night turns into day
…and love takes over.*

Day 18 - Eternal

"Two Became One"

*Two heartbeats
joined as one.*

*Instant love when
we first met.*

*Peace has blown us
into another time.*

*All of the love of the
generations is given to us.*

*Echoes of our love rolls
from soul to soul,
as we travel to the
land beyond.*

Day 19 - A Fine Man

"Just What a Real Woman Needs"

*Into the room he walks
and the stillness overcomes.
Tailor-made from head to toe,
like a new glove that fits
like aged leather.
Something within
moves you to turn.
A gentleman beyond
the word, fresh as coffee
that he wills in
the morning.
Sweet as the berries
he feeds you as you lay.
Softly he calls you a lady,
not because he has to
…because he means it.
He's what every woman wants
He's loving,
Kind, and fine.
But sorry ladies,
    this one is mine.*

Day 20 - A Fool's Love

"Don't Be Fooled"

Time was the beat
that I used to keep
…you loving me.

As the storm grew stronger
we grew weaker
day by day.

You had no time for us
Yet, there was so much
more love to give.

Alone in my bed
the tears surrounded me
but soon faded away.

To you love is a game.
For me it's life
to death do we part.

Real love never lets go.

Stephanie A. Young

Day 21 - Gift

"The Thing That You Cannot Buy"

*Just as I turn my heart to stop,
my mind presents another key,
to an unknown door of love,
when the pain is overcoming me.*

*The taste of love burned my tongue.
I just bite it until I feel no more.*

*There's a place I go to get the
feel of hunger quenched.
It begins on the last road to my
heart and leads to the first spot
of joy, with just one touch.*

*Someday when you wake from your fear.
I will take you to the core of it all.
The beginning of an everlasting wonder,
wrapped in ribbons of love.*

Day 22 - Happy As I Am

"From One Mother to Another"

I gladly go on without your old wisdom.

*I lean not wholly on what you
have passed on to me.*

*Though months have passed and
a year has come and gone, your
morning call still echoes in my memory*

*My bitter days are now brighter and better
so I pass on your remixed wisdom to a
new generation.*

*Every day is a new beginning of learning
and for this I unwillingly thank you.*

Day 23 - The Lust of a Woman

"Control That Should Never Be Given Away"

Just when the burning
is almost over a new hunger
moves in, time brings
your needs closer to wants.

The lady inside will not
let the tramp run wild.

Mindless hours go by
with the night.
The sweat of another
cools your heart.

On the other side
of the door is a joy
that will melt away
the lust and leave
a glow of love.

Day 24 - Tell Me the Truth

"My Vow"

*Now is the time of the
day, month, year;
it's just walk away.*

*There are three beautiful
moments that we have
created.*

*One was the day you said I do.
Two others who are growing
strong and fast every day.*

*Be true to me for love's sake.
Not because you have to but
because you want to.*

*Do unto me. I'll do unto you.
Do what is true and right.
Till death do we part.*

Day 25 - Living Arrangements

"Learning To Love For the First Time"

I hate your stuff. You say mine is too big.
Is this what we have been longing for?
Is it love or just to love a game?
Hours to love, just as many tears.
A few minutes to smile every day.
An ounce of joy to a gallon of trouble.
Friends apart, stranger together.
We give and take until there is no more.
Finally love has come.

The vow of, "till death do we part," will never end.
Suffering was the strength we needed to make love last forever.

Day 26 - Just a Thought

"Fear of love"

Softly I say to myself, "I can't."
You will when I love you.
Boldly, I hope for faith.

I give you all and more,
when I see without a point.
Believe and this shall never end.

Beauty, joy, pain,
love with no other
will ever be the same.

All the fear that surrounds me.
I see no trace when we walk and talk
hand in hand, heart to heart endlessly

Day 27 - My Private Vampire

"Forever Love"

The night was hot and sticky and so was club midnight. Out of the corner of my eye there he was. Tall, dark and I do mean dark.

I saw the ponytail and I prayed, "Lord let this be the finest man in this club". If this is a woman in drag, I'm going to look and feel real stupid. Thank you God!

I don't know why I walked over here. But I saw you and I couldn't stop myself. To my surprise he asked, "Will you marry me?" To my surprised I answered, "Yes."

I didn't believe him until I saw the coffin and the castle. I thought to myself, "So what, he loves me enough not to bite me. We can adopt twins; a boy and a girl, Damon and Dana. I'll do my day thing and he'll do his night thing and still have time to do our thing."

So off to the castle. The Rolls and the family jewels not far behind, safe in my man's coffin.

Day 28 - Time to Finish the Beginning

"Knowing What I Want"

In my life, love has been my only claim to give, to talk of, to live for., and my pain to hunger for but most just to feel it.

I've looked for it in all the wrong places, people and word. I have found it in all the right times, friends, and lovers. But now love has found me cold and alone, in the light of the morning, fresh as the dew.

On the edge of my pain with one touch of a hand, with the kiss of a child looking for nothing. If love can find me, touch me, feel me, and see me for who I am, this is my beginning.

Day 29 - Night Wish

"Peaceful Time of Life"

*Surrounding the day,
pushing the night.*

*Out are the stars
telling tales of old,
hiding is the sun in
a land far away.*

*Moon shining like a
child for a treat fresh
and new every time.*

*Quiet and peaceful,
almost unending.*

*Soon dust will
awaken the dew.*

*A play that unfolds
day in and day out.*

Day 30 - Us

"Tripping Together"

*If you could only see the hunger inside of me,
night after night in this bed of passion.*

*It doesn't want to consume you
just take you to a place that we both can share.*

*I promise never to make you feel weak or small
but build you up big and strong forever in my life.*

*Just around the corner there is a whisper in the air,
to let me know that I can hold out and hold on
and never give up my desires.*

*If you cannot find your love shut your eyes and let
them see what has always been there.*

*Reach out your arms and do what must be done
to free you from yourself.*

*Take the first step into your mind.
Find what fear is there and remove it*

Day 31 - Endless Ribbons of Life

"Traveling Without Grace'"

Born with the life of thousands. Growing with the wind but never fast enough. Loving with the faith of a child. Hating what should not be teaching in my own special way. Learning every minute and hour of the day. Hoping unconditionally.

Praying in the midnight hour, good, bad, happy, or sad. Trust that ends in hurt. Still believing, understanding, and waiting for a new world. Lonely for those who watch over me. Pride and joy keeps me going everyday by those who wish to take without asking.

Wondering if I care enough to help. Trying to use my soul. Learning, knowing what has meaning and value only comes with time and age. Giving only if it feels right. Taking only what I need and knowing what is good. Showing the way only if I know the way. Leaving my mark. Lord, did I pass the test?

Day 32 – Dark Side

"My Best Time"

*The beauty of the night
brings the perfection of love.*

*Hearts obey the laws of
passion.*

*A flame to start a heart,
is just a search way,
coming through the dark.*

*The dark side is just a
like tomorrow.*

*Only dreams can
make it real.*

*All things are possible
to those who believe in
the night*

Day 33 - Just Business

"When I Wasn't Looking"

Believe me when I say,
"Business was my only prize,
when it came to you."
A love job fit for two.

Then in a flash I opened
my eyes and walked into
the truth.

In your arms is a soul
that is filled with the
secrets of love.

In my heart it was
just business, but
your love brought me…
Paid in full.

Stephanie A. Young

Day 34 - Word Journey

"Me and My Pen"

*Inside this room I sit with
pen and paper in hand.*

*I travel to places that come
to me in dreams and fantasies.*

*Dreams that are sweet as love,
unseen but yet to be tasted.*

*Thoughts that feel
my every word.*

*Emotions that you can see
and hear in one breathe.*

*I write because sometimes
 my tongue gets tired,
but my mind has a
heart of its own.*

When My Soul Started To Fly

*It has gone on voyages of
life that I have to deal
in my own time.*

*Fantasies that I create
with the wave, a touch,
a stroke of my pen.*

*I hope someday that they
will lead me to a new world
of never ending journeys.*

Day 35 - A Ten Dollar Visit

"True Friends"

*Today I saw two friends
that I hadn't seen in a long time.
They were almost the same
as I remembered.
One was wise, strong,
steadfast in God,
in love, and happy.
The other searching for
love... finding it, but not
letting it love her.
Still the friends I remember.
As the day ends I sit
and think for $10 of gas,
how much joy this
visit brought me.*

Day 36 - Ageless Veil

"Blessed Living"

*Year after year, time seems
to standstill for some.
Love handles, potbellies,
crow's feet out of sight f
or those who live right.
Smooth, lean, strong, fadeless,
full of youth in reverse.
Minds of steel.
Hearts strong as bucks
running wild and free.
Time and chance is
all that you get.
Long baths, slow
walks, deep kisses.
Go as you came with
an open heart.*

Day 37 - Old Girl

"My Full Blooded Mama"

They said she was a long,
hot drink of water on a cold day.
Sometimes they call me by
her name, and sometimes I answer.
I think to myself, we are more
alike than they ever knew.

If she was here today,
I wonder if she would do
all the things they dislike,
or would she tell all of them
where and when to step off.

On the street I see a face,
that looks like hers and
my soul leaps.
Deep in the night I hear a
voice, and I think,
"Does she see me in this world?"

Day 38 - Old News

"Don't Fall For Everything"

Last year's news,
this month latest,
next week's centerfold.

Now you're just another
pretty face in the crowd.

Chance is the law of life.

If you only look to the past,
you will miss the future.

Time is yours for the taking.

It's easy as dominoes;
one push is all it takes.

Day 39 - Pain in My House

"Stone Hearted"

*With the rising of
the sun, it surrounds
all who are awake.*

*Black hearted, mean
spirited, evil minded,
cold to the bone.*

*My mama said love
Everybody but not
everybody's ways.*

*Every day I pray for
old age and not old
hearted ways.*

Day 40 - Tell Me Who Owns You

"True Gifts"

I'm a slave to your heart. I'm a slave to a child mind and body. This is the payment of life daily, until my last is first, again. In this world all we own is what we have worked for... and now it seems to own us.

The best that we have is still free, if we only stand back and take a look. A big, old, country simple smile, old folk's ways, proud and uncommon thoughts of a road less traveled. Saving all that we have, just to pass it on to start over. Hoping that it would be better and more loved than before.

Now it's my turn but what do I really have to give. My love, my dreams, I pray not my hate. Yes, sometimes my pain. I will be owned only by the love of my God. For this I will always own, joy, hope, and dreams for the next to come.

Day 41 - Unrest

"Words That Trouble Me"

A loss of words is
a first for me.
In the night the words
never seem to stop.
In the dark of my mind
they come to me.
Sometimes they come for me.
Sweet dreams of joy and pain.
They control me with arms
of tears, legs of
soul and wonder.
In the daybreak they
leave me with peace.
I wake from my war with
the angel of dreams.
Only to fight my day dreams.
A never ending war that
I have no choice in.
In this unstoppable
fight I soldier on.

When My Soul Started To Fly

Day 42 - Mary, Do You See What You Got?

'The Half of Me That Will Never End"

I've got a big brother tall, lean, and strong, full of love for those who love him, for others not even the time of day. I've got a baby brother. Some say he is lost, but they don't know what I know. He can see what we don't think to look for.

I've got two sisters. My baby one, people say she's cold but she's not. When she has something to say, we will know. Until then, just wait. Now the other one is like my twin, with skills she hasn't used yet. Colors only she can see and put together.

Don't think I could forget about the new future to the story. With a little flavor of all of us, but mostly all of you. Now me, well I know that you are and always be my mother. Even if I didn't say it much, my heart will never let me forget. See what got, Mary? Love forever.

Day 43 - Pathfinders

"Mindless Travel"

*In the middle of life.
Your heart's mind began
to search for an escape.*

*Night, day,
time, and space,
for the joy of one.*

*One world, love life
of never ending
adventures.*

*Nomads of the
future.
…next stop,
the black hole.*

Day 44 - My Name Is Color

"Just Living"

The job was mine until I didn't have blond hair and blue eyes. The apartment was for rent until I came to sign the papers. Maybe I had too many jobs

The home was in a nice, quiet side of town until we rolled up from the hood. The car was just what we were looking for until the fried chicken and watermelon joke was funny anymore.

The wedding was going fine until grandma said, "Is that the groom or one of the waiters?" We got to heaven and God said, "Come on in. We are all the same up in this camp."

Day 45 - Mother of Words

"Comfort for My Sadness"

As I sit waiting for her, I wondered, "If she had felt the rage of another on her very being, not just her body. Has she lost a love to a big deal with a little name?"

I too have felt my voice become a knife to make me silent. Did she see pain is as color like me? Was her heart stained by life? Is she the truth, answer, or question?

There she is. Some say she is sad. I see her. She's not sad, but alive.

Day 46 - Mama's Cooking

"Food for Life"

Sweet butter in the morning, fried corn at night, it's not just another sweet potato pie, I spy.
- *Long, green, and tender, simmered down collard greens.*
- *Cornbread and crackling, black eye peas, hot pepper with my ice tea.*
- *Fried okra to fight for. The Vidalia that brings tears of joy into your eyes.*
- *Cherry tomatoes that dance from the vine to my mouth.*
- *Macaroni and cheese that melts my mind. Pinto beans until I scream.*
- *Chocolate cake big enough to last for nine days.*
- *Banana pudding on the front porch.*
- *Blackberries from the bush. Peach cobbler in the August heat.*
- *Cucumbers tart enough to be sweet.*

Summer has come and gone and mama's cooking still lingers on my tongue.

Day 47 - I know Who I Was

"Old Hearts"

My heart holds the love of those before me.

In these hands give the healing of things untold from a time of war.

With this mouth, words of passion that ruled an untamed world.

Sound as big as the mountain and as small as a grain of sand.

In the eyes of a child, I have seen the beginning and near end of the magic, we all dream.

Now it starts to make sense.

All I have to do is say it, feel it, and do it.

Then what I need, want, and desire will be mine.

Day 48 - So What If I Got Bills?

"Life Has Its Moments"

So what if we get a chicken leg and the neck down between the three of us. You get the salt and I'll get the pepper and we'll have on heck of a soup.

So what if we got the final notice. Its daylight, we'll just put out the candles. My mama told me I was a real black woman and I didn't the light to see my man.

So what the gas is off. Baby, you get some charcoal and I'll fix you a five course meal and dessert plus a picture of red Kool-Aid.

So the cables off? At least the phones on until the end of the month. Do we have any long distance calls to make?

I love you and you love me, and this little boy is the joy and sometimes pain in our life.

Hey baby, we got any mayo? I feel like a ham sandwich. What about hotdogs, tuna, and some chips?

You got any money?

Stephanie A. Young

Day 49 - Just Another Joker

"Not So Funny After All"

Did you hear the one about...?
Yeah I sure did. I didn't like it then and sure as h#!! don't like it now. I know, I know, you thought it was funny. See, that's the start of it all. Big nose, big lips, big anything and then it's all a good laugh.

I say it, you say it, and when nobodies laughing, it's like a wildfire. Light bright, black, brown, yellow, d@^, near blue. Got to be a joke in there somewhere.

Long, straight, short, nappy, soft, hard, brought in a bag to mean for a comb. But you know what it all means, mind your own business, sweep around your own door.

I hear she's got one on her and one in her. Mama's baby, papa's baby, if the judge says so.

How many holes are they going to put in their heads?

As many as they can hold.

How long did she stay in front of the liquor store? Till God brought her home. Now she's all alone in that little rock. Go ahead, can you make me laugh now?

Day 50 – Hey! …How Are You?

"The Only Daddy I Knew"

"Hey Pops! So today's birthday."
"Pops, who you calling, Pops?"
"That's Mr. Pops to you and I have you know. I still got gas in this tank."
"Okay, old man so you're eighty one years old today. I bet mama can still make you take your pills."
"She can make me do anything. I love her."
"Come on let's go steal a piece a cake."
"Piece? Little girl, I want the whole thing."
"So Pops, tell me what it's like being eighty one?"
"From one to twenty I was young and on fire. From 30 to
40 I found life, God, and your mother. From 50 to 60 I didn't have to pay so many taxes. Oh, now to the good part, I finally got my hand and Uncle Sam's pocket, and it feels pretty good. Hey turn on the heat. I may be eighty one but these bones feel like ninety one and where is your momma?"
"Don't get all crazy. She's somewhere around here. Hey! Look, Pops. There goes your grandson. Mama

can we cut the cake now? Pop says he's getting old just thinking about it. Happy birthday, Pops. Love ya."

Day 51 - My Sister, My Brother

"Family Without A Doubt"

From the first day we met it was the to Miami kids versus the Georgia kids.

Mama threw us together, hoping we would love each other, or just like one another.

Over the years we've all grown to understand just what a family is.

Even with the miles between us, now that mama's gone time spent together is a true thing of joy.

If her eyes are on us, I'm sure she would be glad to see the love that she left here.

A proud grandma's part would be her best role.

Sometimes when my own looks at me in a funny way, I think to myself, "My sister, my brother which one does he look like?"

Day 52- World

"Living As Real People"

First you take my land
then you take me from it
but still I see freedom.
Without my pride
no longer I am human.
Without love, only hate
I now see fear and pain
but I still have a heart.
Hope far and unknowing
time in my Savior's way of
answering all that hold me back
but I still see my reward.
Now and then you take one of us
and we take one of you.
Now that you can't hang me
you have to cheat me.
Now that you can't buy me
you have to sell yourself.
But now that I'm here to stay
know that this is my freedom land
heart, pride, Savior and just reward.

Stephanie A. Young

Day 53 - Me and the Gang

"Friend Till The End"

*Killing time was the
magic of the day,
dancing with my
brothers and sisters,
always around when
I was down and out.
Friendship will never
go out of style.
All those years of
streets and fights.
No one cared more
than you.
Watch and listen for
me light-years beyond.
Live and pray that life
gets better as time goes by.*

Day 54 - A Good Day

"Summertime"

*Morning has come for all to
see and know who is in command.*

- *Rainbows on the hill*
- *Noon day dances*
- *Sweet grass in the breeze*
- *June peaches*
- *Summer fairs*
- *Plays in the park*
- *Water fights*
- *Cookie crumb*
- *Chocolate dreams*
- *Purple evenings surrounds stars bright strong and far.*
- *Midnight rides, rest for the weary, waiting for another good day.*

Stephanie A. Young

Day 55 - The Ghetto That Won't Rub Off

"The Nights When No Man Is Afraid"

As the night creeps in
the evils of the world
come out to play.

There on the concrete jungle
the lambs of God hide
as the wolves gather
for the hunt.

Tonight the fanged ones
have met their match.
The once sleeping warriors
takes a stand and the fight is on.

Finally there's peace
and the land is free for all
The land smiles and reaches
to touch the heart of man.

When My Soul Started To Fly

The sky smiles with the colors
of love and warmth
and wraps itself around
all that stands for truth.

Day 56 - Winters Visit

"First Sight of Winter"

The sun was shining and the wind whistled a low love song.

The frost tickled the grass.

The morning glories danced along the edges of the fence.

The last rose petal drop to the ground and blew a kiss goodbye.

The brown, crisp, elm leaves curled up as if waiting for on an old friend coming home.

The blackbird sailed in on the last wave of air.

The old oak tree reached up as far as he could to say a little prayer.

Winter walked over to his friends and said, "I will not stay long for I have places to discover and very little time to work with. Rest until we meet again."

Day 57 - A Voice That Carried

"Mr. James Wakefield"

As a child my voice was small and weak. As an adult life changed that same voice into a true blessing.

This voice spoke with lightning words of knowledge. This voice spoke of ancient lands and people we descended from.

This voice spoke words of love and graced me with a lifetime partner. That same voice brought me a gift from God now shines their own lights.

For when this voice is to no longer be heard, it shall echo in the hearts, minds, and souls of all that I touched.

Day 58 - Now I Know Better

"I Found Me"

There was a time in my life when I was so low, until I couldn't see up.

As I searched for answers to the question of my life, love and pain seem to come to me hand in hand.

My mind was imprisoned by pain. My body was locked into an emotionless cell but my soul longs to be free.

One cold, dark morning I took a hold of myself. I wrapped my pride and dignity like a bundle of newborn joy, and walk out into the world.

Life is now a joy and blessing. Living is a newfound treasure every day.

Day 59 - Gathering Of Our Hearts

"When You See How Small and Short Life Is"

There on the sandy hills at a small country church we gathered in the name of love and honor; with hearts overjoyed and saddened at the same time.

We stand and give praise to our maker, for the rivers that we have crossed, for the trials that we have shared, for the earthly changes we have seen, and the blessings received.

We gather with old hearts and new, with the hopes of seeing another day, another month, another year of love for one another.

Day 60 - Blessed

"I Am Loved"

Life has shaken me. Joy has replaced my pain.

My path healed by prayer. Hard roads I have traveled. Rough seas I have sailed.

I stand and receive grace and mercy with every day that is given to me.

Even when the darkness encamps me, divine angels usher me into the land of glory.

As the day grows to an end and the earth is small in my sight, I am transformed.

My footsteps are not just a memory. I am beautiful, loved, and eternally blessed.

Works by Stephanie A. Young

Why My Soul Started To Fly is available:

Amazon.com
Destinypublishings.com

For book signing and poetry reading you can contact her at: <u>say444173@yahoo.com</u>

www.ingramcontent.com/pod-product-compliance
Lightning Source LLC
Chambersburg PA
CBHW071332040426
42444CB00009B/2134